For my mother, Gabriela, my father, Miguel, and my sister, Adriana

Henry Holt and Company, *Publishers since 1866*
Henry Holt® is a registered trademark of Macmillan Publishing Group, LLC
120 Broadway, New York, NY 10271 · mackids.com

Our books may be purchased in bulk for promotional, educational, or business use.
Please contact your local bookseller or the Macmillan Corporate and Premium Sales Department
at (800) 221-7945 ext. 5442 or by email at MacmillanSpecialMarkets@macmillan.com.
Library of Congress Cataloging-in-Publication Data is available.

First edition, 2023
Book design by Aram Kim and Marissa Asuncion
Printed in China by Hung Hing Off-set Printing Co. Ltd., Heshan City, Guangdong Province
Artwork created with watercolor, graphite, charcoal textures compiled by digital painting

ISBN 978-1-250-25777-2 (hardcover)
1 3 5 7 9 10 8 6 4 2

BENITO JUÁREZ
FIGHTS FOR JUSTICE

Beatriz Gutierrez Hernandez

GODWINBOOKS

Henry Holt and Company

New York

My name is Benito, and I live in San Pablo Guelatao with my uncle, Bernardino, along with twenty other Zapotec families. Uncle Bernardino took me in after my parents and my grandparents passed away.

I spend my days plowing the earth and herding my sheep around the village and its outskirts. On Saturdays, Uncle Bernardino teaches me some words in Spanish. In Guelatao, Zapotec is the first language, and since there are no schools, learning Spanish is almost impossible.

While I walk my sheep, I hear the sounds of nature and I look at my surroundings. Listening and observing, I read my first book, and I become aware of a conflicting truth: This land of charm that I live in is also home to rejected and forgotten families, to hungry children.

After one of my sheep disappears, I run away. I am scared of facing my uncle, but more than anything, I am eager to see what is beyond Guelatao.

Before the sun sets, I reach the city of Oaxaca. My older sister, Josefa, lives here. She works as a cook for a prominent family, los Maza.

Wandering through endless mazes, I am stunned by loud announcements: "¿Quién quiere enchiladas? ¡Enchiladas calientes!" "¡Vendo petates de tres varas!"

Knocking on door after door,
I am finally met by a familiar face.

A few weeks later, I move in with Antonio Salanueva, a very religious man who is friends with the Maza family. Antonio gives me a job in his bookbinding shop and takes me to school. Immersed in books, I dive into stories of heroes and thinkers, of battles that are won and lost. In the real world, I witness my country being torn by war. But I also watch the battles of people who work hard and earn little.

When the Oaxacan Institute of Arts and Sciences opens up, I beg Antonio to let me enroll in its law program. As he expected me to follow a religious career, he hesitates. The Institute is the first nonreligious school in the city. However, he gives in, with one condition: From now on, I have to fend for myself.

EL SIGLO DIEZ Y NUEVE

After graduating, I become a lawyer. I want to battle the inequality and misery that I first encountered in Guelatao. Plenty of the cases I work with involve Indigenous communities that are being abused, stripped of their lands, and robbed by those who find themselves in powerful positions.

CHURCH PROPERTY

Amid this cloudy trail, I cross paths with the Maza family once more. I fall in love with their daughter, Margarita, who is serious and thoughtful. She says the same about me. And I see such strength in her that it inspires in me a profound trust. We get married, and soon after we start a large family.

Some years later, I become governor of the state of Oaxaca. A group of Indigenous people from my hometown brings me gifts of all sorts. "You understand what we are missing, and you will not forget about us. We don't have anything else to give to you, so take this as a gift in all our names." These words echo in my mind while I lead my people and speak to them. Throughout my term, I build roads, found schools, and open hospitals.

HOSPITAL

ruled several times before takes over the presidency. Santa Anna destroys freedom of the press, unjustly imprisons whoever disagrees with him, and comes up with absurd taxes: for pets, windows, and car wheels, to name a few. My opposing views cause me to get arrested and imprisoned. I am banished to La Habana, where I board a boat to New Orleans to gather with a group of comrades. Exiled and far away from our motherland, we plan a revolution to overthrow Santa Anna's wicked government.

While I'm unable to survive by twisting cigarettes in a tobacco factory, Margarita does not think twice. Back in Oaxaca, she pawns all her belongings and opens up a small convenience store to support our family.

On our return to Mexico, my comrades and I are capable of defeating Santa Anna's rule. Working within the recently established president's cabinet, we begin to draft a series of laws that will be part of a new constitution. As I have witnessed throughout my life, the most vulnerable people have constantly been harassed by certain institutions. And so, I propose a law that intends to get rid of the excessive power held by the church and the army,

SALARIO JUSTO

LIBERTAD DE EDUCACIÓN

LIBERTAD DE EXPRESION

LIBERTAD PARA TODOS

which is then published as the Ley Juárez. Ley Juárez becomes part of the
Leyes de Reforma, which seek to separate the church from the state and aim
for freedom of religion.

The new constitution is published a couple of years later, crystallizing what
was once conceived in New Orleans: We are all free and have the same rights,
and there are no divisions between races. The constitution causes an outrage
among those who are more conservative, who fear that their privileges are
threatened and who are scared of change. Throughout the country,
multiple rebellions emerge.

While I'm working as head of the Supreme Court in Mexico, the country's president, Ignacio Comonfort, decides to void the constitution due to outside pressure—specifically, a rebellious conservative movement led by a general named Félix María Zuloaga. Comonfort is removed, and I am given the presidency as I am second-in-command. Simultaneously, the opposing group proclaims Zuloaga as their president. The endless war that unfolds during the following years will be called the Guerra de Reforma. Throughout these years, I flee Mexico City and relocate to different towns, finally settling down in Veracruz.

Margarita, who has remained in Oaxaca with the rest of our family, has to shelter in a couple of ranches. She then decides to cross the Sierra Madre Mountains of Oaxaca on foot with all our children. She meets me in Veracruz while the harbor is being attacked by conservative troops.

No matter the circumstances, I am firm on establishing the previously proposed Leyes de Reforma. We must keep protecting individual rights, civil liberties, and the rights of our nation. We need to bring peace back to our country and demand progress and equality. My government's forces regain strength bit by bit, finally defeating the opposing army at the Battle of Calpulalpan.

Once again elected president, I find
myself guiding a country hit by
extreme poverty and deeply
ravaged by war. In order to
recover, my government
temporarily pauses a debt owed to
foreign countries. Seeing this as a
transgression, the French Empire sends
its troops to our lands.

Backed and incited by the recently defeated conservatives,
France imposes a European monarch to rule over Mexico.

An Austrian noble and
a Belgian princess arrive in
Mexico City. Maximilian and
Charlotte are crowned emperor and
empress of Mexico. They decide to move
to the Castillo de Chapultepec, where they
hire stage designers to renovate the palace.
Money is squandered on silverware, glassware,
tablecloths, horses, and carriages.

In the midst of the French invasion, I have to flee the capital for a second time. In constant movement from town to town, my cabinet and I head toward the north of the country and continue to lead the government.

As the war devastates the country, I am separated from my family. Margarita and my children are sent to New York, as they are no longer safe in Mexico. Through continuous persecution and unrest, I travel across the northern desert under extreme conditions, trying to resist an invasion that continues to spread across the country. I receive tragic news from abroad: Two of my children have passed away.

Slowly, the enemy's army starts weakening as it begins to withdraw and return to France to fight an imminent war. Our people start regaining strength, and gradually we retake our cities, heading toward the capital. Maximilian, the emperor, is arrested and judged for his crimes against our country's independence and freedom. After the trial, in which Maximilian is unable to prove his innocence, I am begged by countless personalities to pardon him. But I choose to follow my unwavering sense of justice for my country. I make the tough decision to punish him.

Mexico City welcomes me triumphantly after a few weeks. I am greeted by my loving family after years of separation, and I am overwhelmed with euphoria. "¡Viva la independencia!" "¡Viva México!" And to my people, I say, "We have reached the greatest good that we could think of, accomplishing for the second time the independence of our country." I enunciate the words that will be etched into my country's memory:

These last years were a heavy burden on Margarita. Throughout her time in exile, while she was trying to keep our family afloat, Margarita was troubled by anxiety and sorrow. She became ill with an incurable cancer, and consequently she dies. In silence, I suffer from her absence, trying to prevent any emotion from breaking my spirit. But I cannot bear the pain. My health begins to collapse under the grief.

Not long after Margarita's death, taking my usual walk, I wander off. From far away, I see a child looking back at me. Without words, he invites me to follow him through a familiar path.

After
reaching the end of
the road, I stumble upon an
audience of curious faces. With sparks
in their eyes, I can glimpse their excitement
to dive into the world, a place of strange
contradictions. This land of charm, home to
shattered towns and hungry children, is also a
cradle of hope—of deprived children, who with
love and determination can reach everything. Just
like that orphan child who devoted himself to
his people, seeking justice, equality, and
freedom for all.

AUTHOR'S NOTE

Benito Juárez García was born in San Pablo Guelatao, Oaxaca, on March 21, 1806. One of his greatest legacies is the establishment of the 1857 Constitution and of the Leyes de Reforma, which set the path for Mexico's modernization. His own contribution to the Reform Laws, Ley Juárez, ended the "fueros" and privileges of the church and the army. These fueros were exclusive rights that allowed members of both institutions to be cleared from being judged by a regular court. With the Reform movement, Mexico became a secular country. To this point, the church and the government had practically been the same entity for 300 years.

Along with a group of liberal politicians, Benito absorbed the exhaustion of the people and sought to eliminate the remains of the colony. The 1857 Constitution stated that castes would no longer exist and that everyone would be free and have the same rights. The constitution abolished slavery, forbade noble titles, made education free, and established fair pay and freedom of profession. To a country recently coming out of a colonial system, it was a huge breakthrough. This notably progressive movement also caused controversy, which eventually led to the Guerra de Reforma.

Following the Guerra de Reforma, during the French invasion, Benito crossed the desert through extreme conditions, led his presidency while on the run and in poverty, and suffered loss in his family. Despite the losses and lack of resources, Benito's forces did not give up. The triumph over the invasion and the empire meant the success of the democratic system over the monarchy. Benito's motto, "Among individuals, as among nations, respect for the rights of others is peace," acknowledged a universal principle based on a regard for freedom and independence of all nations.

Throughout Benito's life there was always one constant: Margarita Maza. Margarita was a fighter. While Benito was exiled, imprisoned, or on the run, she took care of their family, traveled distances to meet with him, lived in scarcity, and endured the loss of children. Margarita accompanied Benito all the way through, remaining strong for him despite her suffering. She made sacrifices for Benito's cause without ever questioning it. And it was her strength that kept Benito going during the toughest moments.

Often seen as a mythical figure, Benito has become unreachable through time and hard to identify with. But his speeches and writings reflect him as a humble man. He was very intelligent, deeply wise because of his frequent reading, and quite open minded. Benito was consistent with himself and his principles, and incredibly persistent. No matter what, he always aimed for the liberation of the underprivileged, first as a lawyer and later on through the constitution and the Reform. Benito sought freedom from the church, from enslavement, from ignorance, and from exclusion. Since he was a young man, this was his wish, and this is a fundamental truth that we know about him.

BIBLIOGRAPHY

HISTORICAL REFERENCE

Benítez, Fernando. *Un indio zapoteco llamado Benito Juárez.* Mexico City: Penguin Random House Grupo Editorial, 2015.

Benito Juárez García, https://gw.geneanet.org/sanchiz?lang=en&p=benito&n=juarez+garcia. Accessed 1 June 2022.

Henestrosa, Andrés. Los caminos de Juárez. Mexico City: Fondo de Cultura Económica, 2016.

Juárez, Benito. *Apuntes para mis hijos.* Red ediciones S.L., 2016.

Patria. Directed by Matías Gueilburt, narrated by Paco Ignacio Taibo II. Doc & Films Productions, 2019. Netflix.

Peza, Juan de Dios. *Benito Juárez: la reforma, la intervención francesa, el imperio, el triunfo de la República: memorias de Juan de Dios Peza.* Mexico: Editorial Innovación, 1979.

Rosas, Alejandro, and Angélica Vázquez del Mercado. *Cara o cruz: Benito Juárez.* Taurus, 2019.

Salmerón Sanginés, Pedro. *Benito Juárez de su puño y letra.* Mexico City: Instituto Nacional de Estudios Históricos de las Revoluciones de México, 2007.

VISUAL REFERENCE

Barros, Cristina, and Marco Buenrostro. *Las once y serenooo!: tipos mexicanos, siglo XIX.* Mexico City: Fondo de Cultura Económica, 1994.

Barros, Cristina, and Marco Buenrostro. Vida cotidiana: *Ciudad de México,* 1850–1910. Mexico City: Fondo de Cultura Económica, 1996.

Fernández Ledesma, Enrique. *La gracia de los retratos antiguos.* Aguascalientes, México: Instituto Cultural de Aguascalientes, 2005.

Frías y Soto, Hilarión. *Los mexicanos pintados por sí mismos.* Mexico: Librería de M. Porrúa, 1974.

Moriuchi, Mey-Yen. *Mexican costumbrismo: race, society, and identity in nineteenth-century art.* University Park, Pennsylvania: The Pennsylvania State University Press, 2018.

Velázquez Guadarrama, Angélica. *The painting collection of the Banco Nacional de México: 19th century—catalogue.* Mexico City: Fomento Cultural Banamex, 2004.